English Essays & Letters

(For Primary Classes)

AF647125

2

NIDHI SAHNI

SCHOLARS HUB
NEW DELHI

First Published 2009
Revised Edition 2020

Preface

Essays are a means of expressing ones thoughts, feelings and experiences. The words can be woven in such a way that the characters come alive.

The book helps students in building strong language structures through essays, letters and story narration. This will aid students to grasp better knowledge of gathering information, reflecting it well and presenting their ideas in a thoughtful sequence.

Feedback and suggestions are welcome.

Author

Contents

ESSAY WRITING

Part 1 : Our Favourite / Dear Ones

ESSAY WRITING

Part I : Our Favourite / Dear Ones

1. My Father

Like flowers, leaves and branches depend on the tree for their existence, we children are in the same way dependent on our parents. Our father takes care of our home. He is concerned of all the needs of his children, takes them for outings and also helps them in their studies.

My father is an engineer. He is a simple person. He is very polite and loving. He has enabled the construction of many bridges across big cities but does not boast about it. He works till late at night, marking maps for his new projects. I enjoy sitting next to him and filling colours in my drawing book.

My father plays with me like a friend. I climb up on his big and broad shoulders to pluck guavas from the tree in our garden. We enjoy washing our bright new car on Sunday mornings together. My father also plays with me in the rain. My father takes us out for weekly outings every Saturday.

This birthday, he surprised me by visiting my school with lot of gifts for all my friends.

I also want to be like my father when I grow up. My father is my idol.

2. My Little Sister

My little sister is my friend and companion. Her name is Anya. She is a three-year-old cheerful girl. She is popular in the neighbourhood as Tweety, because she is naughty and never stays in one place.

Anya goes to a play school in the neighbourhood. All her teachers like her. She has also many friends in her school. Anya is too young to take care of her bag and books, therefore I make sure to pack her school bag for her.

We go out every evening to play with our friends. I help her on the swings and my friends take turns to give her a ride on their bicycle. My friends like her a lot. At bedtime, I read out stories to her.

One day Anya fell very sick and she was rushed to the hospital. I was worried and prayed for her good health. I was very happy when she came back home well.

Anya will be celebrating her fourth birthday next week. We are preparing for a grand birthday party.

Anya is a very dear sister. She loves me a lot. I thank God for a sister like her.

3. My Dear Friend

Friends are very important in our lives. We can discuss sports, studies and our trips with our friends. Often, we become fond of one special friend among all others. We miss him the day he does not turn up for school. Rohit is my one such friend.

Rohit and I have been studying together since class I. Rohit's father and my daddy work in the same office. Thus, we keep meeting after the school as well.

Rohit is a sharp and intelligent student. He is the favourite of all the teachers. He often scolds me for my poor handwriting. Rohit is a self respecting child. He does not ask for help from anybody and tries to finish his work on his own. He enjoys playing football and has been selected in the school football team.

Rohit has one bad habit. He never finishes his lunch. I always force him to finish his tiffin. We have a big group of friends but Rohit is the best of all.

4. My School

I study in class five in Gyan Mandir School. It is a sixty-year-old school, famous all over the city. It is a big school spread out in a big area right in the heart of the city. Students come from all corners of the city to study in this school.

Colourful rows of flowers welcome us as we enter our school. On one side is a building housing a hundred rooms. There is a big playground in the centre. Rooms have been provided on both sides of the playground to store sports equipment. There are separate courts for Badminton and Tennis. There is a big Activity Hall which is used for assembly and school functions.

All the roads within the school have tall shady trees on both sides. The classrooms are well ventilated with colourful display boards to greet the visitors. There are laboratories for Science, Maths, Geography, Computer Science and others subjects as well. Here we can find all the material related to the respective subject.

Our library is also well stocked with magazines, books, newspapers, and encyclopaedias. There are two staff rooms, a medical room and a canteen.

Our Principal is very strict about discipline. He gives equal importance to sports as much to studies. Our teachers are very devoted and caring. I am very proud of my school and teachers.

5. My Favourite Teacher

Miss Dutta is our science teacher. Her hair is longer than the length of her Kurta. She walks very fast and reaches everywhere in time. She is always full of confidence. Miss Dutta always has a smiling face and greets all the students with affection.

Miss Dutta always explains difficult theory with practicals to make it easy. She also makes experiments fun for us. She answers all our questions well and encourages us to ask more. We call her 'Walking Encyclopaedia' with love.

She has made science a playful activity for us. Science has now become our favourite subject and we like to perform experiments even at home. We enjoy looking at the growing plantlets, the birds, their babies, the rainbow and the water boiling over the burner. The science book also seems to be smiling at us.

6. My Favourite Sport

Sports have a very important role to play in our lives. Sports keep both our mind and body healthy. Health brings happiness. I also enjoy playing games. Cricket is my favourite game. This game was a royal sport in England but it has now become the world's favourite game.

Our school has made arrangements for morning coaching in cricket. This game is played in a big playground. There are two teams with eleven players each. To begin, the captains of both the teams come together for a toss. The one winning the toss decides batting or bowling for his team. The team making a higher score wins the match.

I have practiced everyday to be a good bowler of my school cricket team. But I want to practice more and become a member of the National Team. Sachin Tendulkar and M S Dhoni are my favourite players. I also want to play efficiently like them and become a famous player one day.

7. My Favourite Book

I have been very fond of books since I was young. That time, I used to like books with big pictures. Now I can read well and therefore I enjoy reading books on all subjects.

'Malgudi Days' is my favourite book. This book has been written by R K Narayan and a tele series has also been made on the stories from the book. It is a story about a small boy from a village called Malgudi. His name is Swami. Swami is a naughty boy who always ends up in trouble with his friends. He is very scared of his father who wants him to be a learned man.

Swami does not enjoy studies and likes to explore the world with his friends. I like his exploratory nature. He is an honest child and good to his friends. Swami is very innocent at heart.

Books teach us many good things. They also develop our imagination. While reading stories we feel close to the characters in the story. We should read lot of books, and keep them safely.

8. My Dream / The Aim of My Life

Human beings can reach great heights in their life. We all have an aim for ourselves and we make great efforts to achieve it. We are highly inspired by our elders and we want to be like them.

Though I am very young to decide anything in class V, but I would like to see myself as an Army Officer. I have a strong desire to do something for my country. I feel very disturbed when I hear about militant activities in our country.

I get excited looking at the soldiers in uniform. My grandfather retired from a very high post in Defence.

Everybody respected him a lot. After hearing his incidents of bravery, I also feel inspired to join the Army.

My parents always encourage me in my goal. I also want to study hard and exercise regularly to become capable of fulfilling my goal.

9. My Favourite Country: India

India is the most unique country in the whole world. It is a secular country where people of different faiths live together happily. India even has a diverse natural beauty. The flora-fauna, the forest cover and other scenic beauty is a scientific study in itself.

India has a rich natural resource of snow-clad mountains, depthless oceans, large deserts and thick forests too. Flowing rivers like Yamuna, Narmada, Ganga, Godavari, etc. add to the beauty of our country. Our forests are home to lions, tigers, peacocks, deers, bears, as well as koel, parrots etc.

Our country's soil has given birth to many great saints, dignitaries, scholars and learned men. Swami Vivekanand and Mahavir impressed the world with their philosophy and teachings. Aryabhata discovered 'zero' and taught a new way to the mathematicians across the globe.

Indian universities attract students from all countries. Our doctors are popular for having pioneered many successful life-saving treatments and surgeries. The main motto of Indian thinking is: “Simple living, but high thinking”.

Indian music, dance and cinema is praised all over and has a strong fan following.

I am proud to have taken birth in India, a country complete in all aspects of quality and morality.

10. My Best Holiday

There are many experiences which we do not forget for a long time. Such experiences are very exciting.

One such experience in my life is a short trip to a village resort in Jaipur. It was a two day trip and I can recall every moment of it. It was also my first trip without my parents.

A night before the trip I was not able to sleep out of excitement. On the day of the trip we reached the school at 5 a.m. and boarded the bus to leave for Jaipur. In the six hours of journey we enjoyed dancing, singing and playing games.

We reached our destination in the afternoon. The resort was a true picture of Rajasthan. The colours, the decoration and the hospitality truly depicted the Rajasthani culture. The rooms, furniture, and the huts were a reconstruction of a village from Rajasthan. It was very exciting to sit and sleep on the Charpoys. We rested a while after lunch.

In the evening we went to the fair. It was a fun-filled affair. There were the traditional dancers, camel rides, puppet show and a lavish Rajasthani meal.

The next day after a heavy breakfast and sight-seeing, we left for our school and reached late in the evening. It was an experience which made me feel confident.

11. Our Bus Driver

I am a class V student of Gyan Mandir School. I travel to school by route number 11. This bus carries students of the primary classes only. Since I am the senior most in my bus, the bus driver has made me the monitor. The driver Chandrapal also takes good care of everybody. We feel very special in the bus. We all call him 'Bhaiya' lovingly. He always comes at the right time and never rushes at the bus stop. He carefully notices our behaviour from his rear view mirror. He obeys all traffic rules.

The children initially get scared of his big size and thick moustache but Bhaiya quickly befriends everybody.

Bhaiya always shakes hands with me and calls me his co-driver. I feel very proud of his confidence in me.

12. My Hobby

Hobbies are recreational activities. When we need a break from our daily routine, then we turn to our hobbies.

My hobby is poetry. It is the most imaginative and creative hobby. One takes a trip to a different world while thinking between the lines of a poem. A well rhymed poem is music to ears. One can express one's deep desires and emotions easily through poetry.

Our literature is also enriched by great poets like Surdas, Tulsidas, Mira Bai, Tagore etc. I read their poems constantly to polish my skills.

Poetry has given an outlet to my feelings. Now I find music in all aspects of nature. My poems are regularly published in our Annual magazine. This encourages me to write better and more.

I was awarded personally by the school principal. I was also sent to participate in the competitions in other schools.

I will always be thankful to my mother for inspiring me in my hobby.

13. My Favourite Pet

People always keep fighting amongst each other. None of us has the time to say a few kind words to each other. In such a case, a pet is a wonderful idea. One feels relaxed after spending time with a pet.

I have a fish tank at home. It is a small glass enclosure with a blue plastic roof. The roof holds a light bulb. We have placed a few artificial plants in the tank to give it a natural look. It also has a water filter to keep the water clean and an air pipe to supply oxygen.

I have bought six goldfishes for my tank. They are very naughty. I feed them at the same time everyday. They have naturally become aware of their time of feed and thus begin to swim near the opening of the tank.

I enjoy sitting next to the tank and watch them swim. Sometimes one fish appears to chase another, it is exciting to watch them play.

We clean the fish tank every month and also put medicines in it. Whenever a fish dies, I feel very sad. We remove the dead fish with a net. Fishes have become my best friends and they also respond to my care. They come towards me whenever I am close to the tank. It is a beautiful relationship.

14. My Favourite Neighbour

Dr. Ranjan is our closest neighbour. He has been staying here for many years now. He has a son, Vibhor, of my age and his wife is also a doctor.

Dr. Ranjan is a very busy doctor, but aunty often visits us. Vibhor is my best friend and we always play together in the evenings. We always share our school events.

One night my younger brother fell ill. He was running high temperature and it was raining heavily outside. My father hesistantly called up Dr. Ranjan. He instantly came over and investigated my brother. He gave him medicines and sat by his side all night to see his response. Next morning, as he left for work, aunty joined my mother. She also helped me get ready for school.

With good neighbours by our side, we escaped a big problem with ease. We will always be thankful to them.

15. My Favourite Fruit

Fruits have always been the food of the sages. It is believed that our diet adds colour to our thoughts. Fruits and berries are pure foods instilling pure thoughts. They supply our requirement of minerals and vitamins and also make us capable of fighting infections.

There is a wide variety of taste and colours in fruits. I enjoy eating sweet fruits and I find mangoes most irresistible.

Mango is a summer fruit and since childhood, I always wait for the summer season. My favourite picture always used to be a golden mango with a long green leaf. I get so engrossed in eating mangoes that my clothes carry the tales forever.

Indian mangoes are very tasty. They are also famous world wide. The raw mango drink called 'panna' saves us from the hot dry summer winds. Summers are also the season for mango pickles. They keep the flavour of mangoes alive all year through.

Part 2 : Seasons

16. Winters

India is a country of changing seasons. From the month of October, one can feel the cold coming in. After a long summer, the cool breeze brings a respite for everybody, but slowly all of us seek warm refuge, as the temperature lowers.

The winters are marked by short days and long nights. The sun rises late in the morning and its heat also reduces with intense winters, mountains observe snowfall which also adds to the cold temperatures in the plains. Winter mornings often witness thick fog.

Winters also brings along fruits like oranges, which are rich in vitamin C. Carrots, spinach and other green leafy vegetables are rich iron sources and help us build immunity. People enjoy peanuts while basking in the sun. Hot drinks like coffee, tea and milk are enjoyed with dry fruits.

Unfortunately, winters are a bad time for the poor. They already have poor diets and their poor clothing makes them victims of illnesses. It will be a good gesture to donate our old woollens to these deprived people.

For the well-off families, winters are a carnival time. They play many winter sports on snow clad mountains. They also organise bonfires.

I also enjoy the cold winter months.

17. Spring Season

Each season is marked by different qualities. Spring season is called the king of all seasons. The reason is the outstanding beauty of nature at this time.

February and March bring spring with them. Life begins to gain activity as the influence of winters begins to reduce. The days and nights become almost equal. New leaves appear on the trees. Birds make nests and prepare for their young ones. Beautiful, fragrant flowers fill the surroundings and invite bees and butterflies.

A morning walk in the pleasant spring morning is great for health. With the cool breeze, one feels active and energetic.

The festival of Basant Panchami adds flavour to this season. It is a day of fairs, kite flying and colourful bright dresses. People worship Goddess Saraswati and offer yellow sweets.

Spring is the season of excitement, joy and celebration. Many beautiful poems and songs have been composed on this season. I also prepare my garden every year to welcome spring.

18. Summer

Summer season is the longest season in our country. The hot rays of the sun cover the earth from the end of March to September.

The effect of the sun's heat can be seen the most on the plants and the surface of the earth. The land dries up and develops cracks, the plants droop and the leaves loose their sheen. The heat of the sun is also capable of causing forest fires.

The animals and birds can be seen near water bodies, though the afternoon sky is still and clear.

We like to keep cool with icecreams, lime water and other cold juices. While coolers, air conditioners etc. provide respite from the heat, they also increase the demand and hence the problem of power supply. The schools are shut down in the peak summer months. This is usually the time, people take to hill stations for a break.

We wear cotton clothes in summers and refresh ourselves in the gardens during evenings. The hot, dry winds blow in North India, helping the mangoes to become sweeter. I like summers as I can eat plenty of icecreams, mangoes and puddings.

19. Rainy Season

Every person likes different seasons. My favourite is – Rainy season.

The earth and all the living beings enliven with the first showers after the hot summers. Dark clouds cover the sky and cool breeze makes the surroundings pleasant and cheerful. The peacocks dance at the sound of thunder.

The rains bathe the earth completely. A bright green colour shines on the plants. The roads appear clean and washed. The rivers and streams flow with a new zeal. The frogs and crickets add to the music.

The rains are generally followed by a rainbow in the sky. The combination of a rainy day and tea-pakoras tastes the best.

While rain is very important for life, excess rain brings floods. Rainy season is also a time for water borne diseases like jaundice and cholera. Therefore, we must take care of hygiene especially during rains.

Part 3 : Our National Festivals

20. Republic Day (26 January)

India was declared a republic on 26 January, 1950. The constitution of India was implemented for the first time after a long British rule. It was this achievement which made our independence complete.

26 January is our National festival and a national holiday. The national flag is hoisted at various places on this day. Many cultural programmes are also organised.

A grand parade is organised in the capital city of Delhi. The President hoists the national flag and salutes the parade at India Gate.

The three arms of the Indian Defence display their arms and weapons. School children present interesting folk dances. Many states and departments of the government present tableaus to display their achievement.

The President awards the brave soldiers and children. The Rashtrapati Bhawan is lit up at night.

Our Republic Day reminds us our duties. We should all aim to be responsible citizens.

21. Independence Day (15 August)

15 August is the day of Indian independence. It was after a long battle against the British rule, which was won in 1947. It required the sacrifice of many freedom fighters. This day is celebrated with great joy and is celebrated as a national holiday.

The Prime Minister hoists our national flag and addresses the nation from the Red Fort. The flag is also given a salutation of 21 artillery shots.

The Independence Day is celebrated in all schools across the country. Cultural programmes are organised and the national flag is hoisted with great respect.

The chief attraction of this day is kite flying. The sky over the cities and towns is covered with big and small, coloured kites.

This day reminds us of the martyrs and encourages us to always work hard for our country.

22. Gandhi Jayanti (2 October)

Gandhi Jayanti is celebrated to mark the birth anniversary of the Father of our nation, Mahatma Gandhi. He was born in an affluent family in Rajkot in the year 1869 on 2nd October. His parents were Karamchand Gandhi and Putlibai. Mahatma Gandhi's full name was Mohandas Karamchand Gandhi.

Gandhiji was married at the age of 13 to Kasturba Gandhi. He proceeded to England to complete his education in law. Once he visited South Africa for a law case, and felt humiliated at the treatment given to Indians. He organised a 'Satyagrah' and won a lot of support.

When he returned to India he plunged into the war of Independence with the tools of non-violence and satyagrah. He banished foreign goods and clothes and encouraged all to accept khadi. He was a great social reformer. He worked against social evils like untouchability, sati etc.

It was with his efforts that India gained independence in the year 1947. On 30 January, 1948, Nathuram Godse killed him with a bullet shot.

A prayer meeting is organised every year at the Rajghat on this day. A photo exhibition is also organised. Gandhiji's life inspires us to believe in 'Simple living high thinking'.

23. Children's Day (14 November)

Children's Day is celebrated every year on 14th November. It is celebrated to mark the birth anniversary of Pandit Jawaharlal Nehru. Nehruji was very fond of children and he always celebrated his birthday with children. After his death, 14th November began to be celebrated as Children's Day.

Special programmes are organised in schools every year on this day. Fairs and carnivals are also organised at many places. Many competitions are also organised for children. The schools also award bright students.

The children offer flowers at Shantivan, Nehruji's memorial on this day.

Nehruji believed that children are the future of every nation and therefore we must work together for their education. The society should be rid of evils like child exploitation and child labour.

Years after independence, we are still trying to fight against these evils.

Part 4 : Our Festivals

24. Lohri

Lohri is a festival celebrated on 13th January, chiefly in the Punjab region. The regions of North India, especially Punjab face severe cold. The effect of winters begins to decrease after Lohri. This festival is chiefly related to harvest festivities.

The children go from one house to another singing songs in praise of 'Bhula Hatti'. He was a Robinhood of the area. These children are welcomed with sweets in every house.

The festival is celebrated at night by lighting a huge bonfire. The friends and relatives seat around this bonfire singing folk songs and perform 'gidda'. They also offer sesame sweets and popcorns in the bonfire.

The main delicacies of this festival are 'corn paranthas' and 'mustard saag'. Lohri becomes special for homes with newly wed couples and new born babies.

The festival marks the ending of winters and onset of harvest season.

25. Basant Panchmi

Basant Panchmi declares the arrival of spring after winters.

Leaves and flowers fill up the trees. This festival arriving in February-March fills up the environment with colours, enthusiasm and energy.

Children wear new clothes and enjoy kite flying. The yellow colour is very significant on this day. People wear yellow clothes. They worship Goddess Saraswati with yellow flowers, turmeric and yellow sweets. People pray for knowledge and wisdom as they worship Goddess Saraswati.

According to Hindu mythology, Saraswati sits on a white lotus in white clothes with a veena in one hand. She also holds a holy book in the other hand.

This day is celebrated in many different ways all over the country.

26. Holi

India is a country of festivals. The Indian calendar is full of festivals from all religions and castes. Festivals add colour to our dull routines.

Holi is a festival of the spring season. It is celebrated in March and fills the environment with colours.

According to a story that explains the origin of Holi, a god-loving boy Prahlad was born to a demon Hiranyakashyap. He was a devotee of Lord Vishnu, unacceptable to his father.

The demon's sister sat in a pyre with the little boy in her lap, to burn him alive. She had the boon to survive fire. But, miracle happened. Fire did not touch Prahlad and instead Holika was burnt. Thus, a night before Holi, a bonfire is lit to celebrate the devotion of Prahlad.

People make friends on this day. They wish each other with 'gulal' and sweets. People dance in the streets singing and wishing each other, Children enjoy splashing water on each other with fancy squirts.

Some people use harmful chemical colours and water filled balloons. These can be extremely dangerous. I prefer to play with only natural colours.

27. Id

India is a secular country. People celebrate festivals of all religions with equal joy and fervour. Festivals bring excitement in our lives.

Id is the most important Muslim festival. It is celebrated after a month of fasting called Ramzaan. Muslims observe strict rules and do not eat or drink anything until sunset.

On this day people wear new clothes. Men offer prayers in the mosque. They serve sweet sewain and say 'Id Mubarak'. The markets are flooded with gifts. Fairs and carnivals are also organised.

The children ask 'Idi' from their elders and get gifts, toys and money in return.

Celebrating all festivals together will strengthen our national unity.

28. Rakshabandhan

Rakshabandhan is a symbol of love and affection between the brother and sister. It is a festival of the month of 'Shravan' according to the Hindu calendar and comes on the full moon day.

According to an old tale, when Indra was set to wage a war against Demons, his wife tied a thread on his wrist to pray for his success and he won. Since then, sisters tie Rakhi on their brother's wrist and pray for their success and long life. The brothers in return promise to always take care of their sisters.

The markets are well stocked with colourful rakhis, a month in advance. There are little toy rakhis for little brothers. The markets also stock gifts for brothers and sisters.

On the day of rakhi, brothers and sisters dress up in new clothes. The sisters tie rakhi and give their brothers sweets. They also exchange gifts.

This is a festival of strong relations and is celebrated with great enthusiasm amongst Hindus.

29. Janamashtmi

Hindu mythology has many stories of incarnation of God. Janamashtmi is also a day to celebrate the birth of Lord Krishna, an incarnation of Lord Vishnu. It is celebrated throughout the country with great joy and fervour.

The demon king of Mathura, Kansa, heard a divine announcement on his sister's wedding. Her eighth son would be his slayer. Thereafter he prisoned the newly weds and killed every child born to them. The eighth child, born at midnight, was safely transported to Nand in Gokul.

The 'bal-lilas' and 'ras-lilas' of Lord Krishna has lured our hearts for years. The temples on Janamashtmi carry images from both. The people fast until midnight when they celebrate the birth of Lord and offer sweets.

The festival is celebrated with most enthusiasm in Mathura and Vrindavan. In Maharashtra, pots with butter and money are hung high up in streets. These are reached through pyramids made by young boys.

30. Ganesh Chaturthi

Lord Ganesha is the God of prosperity and wisdom. His birthday is celebrated as Ganesh Chaturthi. This festival comes in the month of August-September.

Ganesha is the elephant God. He was born out of divine powers of Goddess Parvati. Once she asked him to guard while she was bathing inside. At that time Lord Ganesha did not even allow Lord Shiva to enter. Angry, he beheaded Ganesha. When Parvati explained the birth of Ganesha, Shiva asked his disciples to rush for a head. They returned with an elephant head. Ganesha stood up once again. Shiva blessed him that none of the auspices will be complete without first worshipping Ganesha.

This festival is chiefly celebrated in Maharashtra. People make huge 'Pandals' with big idols of Lord Ganesha. They worship and offer sweets to Ganesha, morning and evening. On the day of Ganesh Chaturthi these idols are immersed in the sea.

People pray for prosperity and knowledge on this day.

31. Onam

Onam is a festival of dance, music, delicacies and celebration. This festival is celebrated for four days in the honour of King Mahabali.

People decorate their houses with beautiful rangolis. They make many mouth-watering dishes and organise a grand feast. It is believed that by appeasing Mahabali with this feast, they will be granted prosperity.

The ancient tale says that once Lord Vishnu called on Mahabali who was a proud king. Lord Vishnu came in the form of 'Vaman Dev' and asked for three footsteps of land in donation. When the King agreed, Lord Vishnu increased his size and measured the earth in one step, the sky in the second and placed his third step on the King's head and sent him to nether land.

This festival is especially celebrated in Kerala. People organise boat races on this day. The boats are well decorated and rowed by ten or more people.

The preparation for Onam is a celebration in itself. Such festivals bring joy and fervour in our lives.

32. Vijayadashmi / Dussehra

Our culture teaches us that whenever evil and injustice begin to torment the earth, God takes human form to bring back justice and order. Ravana a demon king began to humiliate the followers of God. Lord Vishnu took birth in Ayodhya as Rama and killed Ravana on Dussehra.

Lord Rama was the son of King Dashratha of Ayodhya. In order to honour the promise made by his father, Rama went for fourteen years of exile. His wife and brother Laxmana accompanied him to the forest. Ravana kidnapped Sita and kept her in his kingdom

Lanka. With the help of the monkey army, Lord Rama brought his wife back.

Ten days before Dussehra, Ramlila is staged in different parts of the country, in which many episodes of Lord Rama's life are played. On Dussehra huge effigies of Ravana, his son Meghnad and brother Kumbhkarna are erected in big grounds. At sunset they are set afire and are burnt down after a series of fireworks. People gather in huge numbers to see this amazing sight.

Dussehra inspires us to believe in truth and justice. It also encourages us to serve our duties and respect our elders as Lord Rama did.

33. Deepavali

Deepavali or Diwali is the festival of lights which is celebrated on the moonless night of the month of Kartik. It is a sacred Hindu festival which reflects our culture and devotion to God.

After fourteen years of exile, when Lord Rama, Sita and Laxmana returned to Ayodhya, they were welcomed with rows of lighted diyas. Since then the ritual of lighting our houses, shops and temples continues.

People prepare for the festival by cleaning up their shops and homes.

They exchange gifts and sweets amongst friends and relatives. Dhanteras is celebrated two days before Deepavali. Buying new utensils on this day is considered very auspicious.

People wear new clothes on this day and light up their homes. They worship Lord Ganesha and Laxmi. The children enjoy bursting crackers on this day.

Some people disrespect this day by gambling and drinking alcohol. We should avoid all this. Deepavali is the favourite festival of all.

34. Christmas

Every religion has some important festivals. These festivals represent the culture and tradition of that religion. The important Hindu festival is Deepavali, that of Muslims is Id and the chief Christian festival is Christmas.

The festival of Christmas celebrates the birth of Lord Jesus, who was born on 25 December in a cowshed.

Christmas is celebrated in many countries around the world. Mass prayers are organised in the Churches. People decorate the Christmas tree at home. They wear new clothes, bake cakes and other dishes. They buy and exchange gifts amongst friends and relatives. At night children wait for Santa Claus to come and grant them their wishes.

Lord Jesus gave shelter to many abandoned people. He healed their wounds and taught them to be kind. He spread the message of brotherly love and affection.

Part 5 : Visit / Trip

35. A trip to the Zoo

A warm sunny day in winter season is perfect for a long trip to the zoo. I carried my water bottle and my mother packed a small lunch for us. Together we set off for the zoo.

The Delhi Zoo is very big. We need at least two hours to take a complete round of the zoo. For those who cannot walk for long distances, electricity driven vehicles are available. We preferred to walk around.

We first saw water birds. There were ducks, swans, herons etc. enjoying the flow of the stream. Then there was a huge fence which housed a hippopotamus. It was being fed fresh grass. His thick skin and heavy body amazed everybody. We then saw the langur, the parrots, owls, jackal, crocodile and deer.

As we reached the tall giraffe, I was amazed to see its height. It was feeding from a big basket hanging from the trees.

The zoo also had elephants, monkeys and white tigers. We took pictures of all the animals but did not feed them at all.

At the end of the trip we enjoyed our lunch in the lush green lawns and then left for our home.

36. A day at the Circus

We live in a big city. Many circus and fairs are organised here. I enjoy circus the most. This time the famous Bombay Circus came to our city. After a week of settling down, they began their shows. My father promised to take me to the circus on Sunday.

We quickly had our breakfast and left for the circus on Sunday. The ground was crowded with people. We bought the tickets and settled down in the front rows.

Soon the bands began to roar and in came a group of red nosed clowns. They jumped around and amused everyone with their pranks. Then the trapeze artists came to display their acts. We were amazed to see their long jumps.

It was now time for the ferocious tigers, lions and cheetahs. Harilal Master raised his hunter and the animals bowed and jumped through a ring of fire.

The circus also showed rare foreign parrots. They could add, subtract and multiply.

All the characters of this circus are always dressed in beautiful and colourful clothes. I liked the circus a lot.

37. A Picnic

To take a break from our dull routine, we decided to go to a peaceful park for a picnic.

On a pleasant Sunday morning, my mother packed our food in a picnic basket. My sister and I packed our toys and my father helped us put everything in the car.

Far from the city, we reached a river side. After settling down, we jumped around and chased butterflies. It was a pleasure to walk on the soft green grass. The cool breeze and the fragrance of wet mud on the river side filled in us a new zeal. We could see a variety of birds of different colours and sizes.

We enjoyed our lunch and set out for the boat ride. As the boat slowly moved away from the banks, the view on both sides kept changing. The clear sky above and flowing water below was an amazing experience. We then played on the swings in the park.

As the sun was about to set, we were forced to pack and bid adieu to this beautiful place. But we will surely return to enjoy this beauty again.

37. A trip to the mountains

The summer season in northern India pushes everyone towards the cooler mountains. Though some people also go to the mountains to enjoy winter sports. We also planned a trip to Nainital in our summer vacations.

We left Delhi early in the morning and reached Nainital in eight hours. The beauty of the landscapes on the way was untouched.

Nainital is a small town built around a beautiful lake. All the hotels are located around this lake. The reflection of the high mountains around can be seen in the lake below.

As we went for the boat ride, the cool breeze refreshed us again after the long journey.

We visited a small zoo nearby and the rock garden. There were many restaurants and shopping places along the Mall road. We enjoyed and stayed at this beautiful place for two days.

After enjoying the fresh air, we were ready to leave for warm Delhi again. We plan to visit this beautiful place again next year.

39. A day at the Cinema hall

The school organises picnics, carnivals etc. to give students a break from studies. Our annual exams were close and our headmistress organised a movie for all of us.

It was a cartoon film based on the life of Lord Krishna. We reached the cinema hall in our school bus. Inside, each row was allotted for a different class. We were also given a complimentary box of popcorn and a glass of cold drink.

As the film began, the lights in the hall began to dim. There was complete darkness around us and we could see only the screen.

The film described the birth of Krishna, his fight with the demons and the slaying of Kansa. It was a beautiful movie with true to life characters.

As the movie got over, all of us were presented paper crowns with peacock feathers.

On Monday a representative from each class thanked the headmistress with a small 'Thank You' card.

40. A trip to Deepavali Fair

An annual Deepavali Fair is organised in our colony ground on the weekend before Deepavali. A specially formed committee takes charge of it. There is an entry fee for the fair, and yet people gather here in large numbers.

We also reached the fair and were thrilled to see its grandeur. There were stalls all around decorated with colourful paper and lightings. Some stalls displayed games, some eatables and others had things for selling. There was a giant wheel right in the centre of the fair.

We enjoyed chaat, then noodles and then the famous chuski. We also played the ring game, the juke box and the dice. There was a wonderful magic show and camel ride. We bought candles, diyas and decorations.

It was late in the evening now and we ended our trip with hot milk and jalebi.

41. A day at the Book Fair

Book lovers will always find a book fair very adventurous. The Delhi Book Fair is a very big fair organised annually. It caters to all interests and age groups. I have always been very fond of books since childhood. Therefore, I try to visit this fair every year.

My mother took me to the fair on Friday, after school. It was organised at Pragati Maidan in Hall No. 8, 9, 10 and 11. There were colourful books all around. Adults and children were flipping through the pages of different books everywhere.

We laid our hands on a few colouring books. There were books on wild birds and animals. Then we reached the cooking stall. My mother bought a few books from there. We then bought a few workbooks on English and Hindi.

There were stalls of creative games as well. I picked up games on word building and mathematics. There were many interesting CDs on stories and rhymes. We bought a few as birthday presents.

After a heart-filled trip to the book fair, we enjoyed snacks at the fast-food joint and returned home.

42. A Train Journey

The giant aeroplanes, the swirling trains and the ships ascending in the deep sea always fill our hearts with excitement. When a mere look of these transports is so exciting, then how adventurous would a ride be.

When my father showed us the train tickets to Agra, I was very happy. We quickly packed and reached New Delhi railway station to catch the Shatabdi. The station looked like a swarm. There were heads everywhere. In between, red shirts with luggage on their heads could be seen rushing in and out.

Our train was right on time. We seated ourselves in the AC chair car and looked outside. There were many stalls selling tea, pakoras, toys, magazines etc. Salesmen kept moving in and out of our coach selling magazines, chips, chocolates etc. They had a very peculiar accent.

Suddenly we felt a jolt. My father told us that the engine had attached. Then a whistling sound came and the train moved. As the train picked up speed, a rhythm seemed to play on the tracks.

Between beautiful sceneries outside, we were served snacks. The trip to Agra was short but adventurous.

43. A trip to the Village

A village is where the nature dwells on its own, away from the pollution of the cities. India has many villages located around our national highways, between every two cities. I also got a chance to see such a village, very closely.

We were on a trip from Delhi to Mussoorie. Suddenly, we had to stop to change a flat tyre. In an attempt to do so, my father misplaced a nut. We decided to search for a mechanic in the nearby village.

As we reached closer, the fragrance of melting jaggery filled the air. We could see small urns and jaggery vendors.

Further ahead, women were drying cow dung cakes over hay. These cakes are used as cooking fuel in the villages. At the centre of lush green fields were tubewells irrigating the crops. We asked for a mechanic from a person in a cowshed. He greeted us with a glass of fresh milk and showed us the way. Treading through kutcha/straw houses we lost our way again. A man personally guided us to the mechanic and also handed over a bag of raw mangoes. We could not refuse his polite gesture.

We finally found the mechanic and took him to the car. I narrated the events and the kindness of the villagers who helped us to reach him. We soon drove off but I felt a deep desire to return again.

44. My first day in School

The school days are the most cherished days of our lives. Our lives always carry the fragrance of our childhood mischiefs.

I always feel that my first day in this school was the most adventurous day of my lie.

I took admission in class V on March 31, 2008. The popularity of this school had always impressed my father. On the first day, I was waiting outside the Principal's office with my father. As we were called in, I could not take my eyes off the numerous trophies in her room. She welcomed and encouraged me and wished me luck for this new experience.

Mr. Sushil was teaching science in the class. He introduced me to the students and made me sit next to a bright child.

By lunch time, I had made friends with everybody. We had lunch together and I was very much a part of the school. As the day came to an end, I had visited all activity rooms with my friends and learnt the names of all teachers. It was a wonderful experience for me.

45. A Rainy Day

Childhood is a careless, naughty time. At times we really enjoy doing things that we are scolded for. Jumping in puddles during rains is just an adventurous activity like this.

My school is close to my house and thus, I walk down myself after school. It was a bright sunny day, but it suddenly began to rain heavily by the afternoon. I had already reached the school gate and there I sought refuge in the guard's room.

My friend and I gazed at the raindrops dancing on the road and were eager to do a rain dance.

We went out on the road and played with our ball. We then followed the tiny streams along the road until we met other boys from the neighbourhood. It was a good time for cricket. We were engrossed in our game and lost track of time. Suddenly I saw my mother under her bright pink umbrella, looking everywhere. My friends immediately fled the scene and I was scared.

She looked at me once and smiled. Surprisingly, she folded her umbrella and enjoyed the rain with me. We danced our way back home and had hot pudding.

46. How I celebrated Diwali

Deepavali is a festival of light, hope and devotion. It represents the Indian culture and beliefs. By celebrating our festivals we offer respect to our culture.

Deepavali was first celebrated on the arrival of Lord Rama in Ayodhya. Following the same custom we clean up our houses and surroundings and light up our homes. I also helped my mother in decorating our house. We made beautiful rangolis outside and exchanged sweets with our neighbours. Everybody greeted us very warmly.

In the evening I put on new clothes and joined my parents for the prayer. I relished the sweets offered as prasad. To avoid pollution our neighbourhood decided to burst very few crackers in the colony ground.

We all lit up our houses with diyas and candles and gathered in the ground. Everyone was given a chance to light a few fireworks. It was great to see colours filling up the night sky.

We had also organised a grand feast after the show. It was fun to celebrate Deepavali with everybody.

47. A night without power supply

We all generally after our dinner, watch one or two programmes on the television and sleep peacefully in our homes. But on one September night, at around 9 pm, there was a power cut. The generators of the society failed and required long servicing hours.

The elders impatiently paced up and down the society roads. Gradually, we also gathered in the society ground. It was a moonlit night with cool breeze. With the noise of children the night soon resounded like the day.

First we lit candles to play musical antakshari, then we decided on hide and seek. It was my turn to catch the others and it was impossible in the dark, I gave up.

Then we shared horror stories. Everyone was getting nervous when suddenly the society lit up again. We all shouted at the surprise. We realised it was past midnight and we all had school the next day.

We ran inside and fell asleep immediately.

48. When the teacher was absent

Our routine in the school strictly follows a time-table. It is difficult to make sudden changes in absence of one teacher.

Yesterday, our English teacher was on leave. Three out of seven classes were of English and this gave us a lot of free time.

If a teacher is on leave, a substitute teacher takes her classes. Mrs. Mili, our music teacher was sent to our class. Our dull English classes were suddenly filled with excitement and music.

Mrs. Mili asked us to close the doors and windows lest we would disturb others. We were then divided into two teams and we played the alphabet game on poems. My team won.

Then she taught us another game. She would give a word to one of us and we would compose two lines on it. Initially, it was difficult but then all of us turned into poets. Archana scored the highest.

We carried the poetic fever to our homes as well.

Part 6 : Health Related

49. Health and Our Life

We can enjoy the gifts around us only if we have a healthy body. A healthy body is always happy and cheerful. If we fall ill then it makes us dull and sad. While, going out in the fresh air excites everyone.

A healthy body is like a gift which we have to maintain ourselves. And to do this we have to make certain rules for our life. Exercise and sports should always be a part of our lives. It is important to work on them regularly.

Our food also has an important effect on our lives. Fried and spicy foods are digested slowly and they keep us uncomfortable for hours. It also leads to many diseases. Green vegetables, fruits, milk, pulses, eggs etc. keep our body healthy and disease free. They also make us alert and active.

The greed for food and laziness are the main enemies of our body. We should try and win over them.

50. The importance of Sports

A healthy body adds flavour to our lives. Like a working machine, our body parts should always be in motion or else illness will deteriorate our body like rust destroys a machine.

Sports are a cheap source of health, energy and recreation. Sports also inculcate qualities like patience and cooperation.

Teams have players from different castes and communities, who have only one goal in common – victory.

The emphasis on sports in schools has been constantly increasing and thus it has now been included as an essential part of the school curriculum. The mind does not develop only through books. It needs active recreation as well.

All students cannot be great sports persons, thus, we should select sports according to our interest and calibre. This is why schools include multiple sports events at all times.

51. Benefits of Exercise

We have heard a million times that 'Health is Wealth'. Because of this we can enjoy other things in life. We can concentrate on our studies also in a healthy state. Exercise is the best means to keep ourselves active and energetic.

Morning walk, swimming, yoga, sports like cricket, badminton, kabaddi etc. are all means of exercises. We can select any of these according to our interest and level. It is important that whatever means of exercise we select, we should be regular in that.

Exercise keeps our body in shape and avoids obesity. It also improves blood circulation. Our body stretches out and muscles loosen up.

Before beginning any form of exercise, one should follow some precautions. We should stop if we feel any strain or pain. Always exercise under the guidance of an expert trainer.

52. Healthy Food

As the weather changes, the newspapers are filled with two kinds of news – the symptoms of seasonal diseases and the list of foods to boost immunity. The main reason is that our food is directly related to our health and immunity.

Students need to concentrate on their studies and thus need to have better immunity. Their diet should have protein rich food like pulses, eggs, meat, soyabeans etc. Foods like chapati, rice and cereals along with limited amount of ghee and butter are good sources of energy.

Students generally sit and study. Thus, they should avoid fried and junk food. These increase obesity and chances of bone related problems.

Green vegetables, fruits, fish etc. boost our immunity. They have essential minerals and vitamins.

Healthy food is the basis for a healthy lifestyle. Sometimes we enjoy junk food as well but these only satisfy our taste buds and nothing else.

53. Morning Walk

An early riser is an alert and active person. It is also said in our scriptures that an early riser gains energy from the sun. The fresh morning rays and the chirping birds fill us with zeal. This is a priceless key to good health.

The people going for morning walk benefit from the pollution free air. This adds briskness to their walk. This time also calms our mind and keeps it so throughout the day.

Morning walk keeps our body youthful. Older people energise themselves through morning walks.

The beautiful morning scenes reduce stress and increase our concentration. Regular walks improve the capacity of our brain, especially improving performance in the examinations.

Thus, the morning walk benefits the body and mind alike.

Part 7 : Science Related

54. Miracles/Contributions/Gifts of Science

We are living in a scientific era where our lives are influenced by constant modernisation. Today the air, water and even the universe are within our reach. Science has made our lives easy and comfortable. Radio, television, refrigerator, telephone are just a few gifts from science.

Today the means of transport are constantly improving. Aircrafts are carrying passengers and cargo over long distances. The improving speed of trains are constantly reducing the distance between two cities.

Telephone, internet, world phone etc. have made means of communication fast and cheap. Through television and satellite we can be constantly in touch with the events around the world.

New inventions and discoveries in the field of medicine have made it possible to cure most diseases known to mankind.

Science in the service of man will always prove beneficial.

55. Computer

The human knowledge bank is constantly expanding. But the limited mental and physical capacity makes it difficult to keep an account of all developments. This human need led to the development of computers.

Computers have become an inseparable part of all areas of life. It can perform long calculations with zero error.

Computers are being used for travel reservations, in hospitals to diagnose diseases, in banks to keep account of everyday transactions. We all prefer to go to 'technically advanced' banks and hospitals which provide quick service.

Computer science has also been included in the school curriculum to make the students better equipped for the modern world.

For most competitive examinations the results are checked by computers. They are used in weather reporting, elections, satellite control, designing clothes, furniture homes etc.

Internet is another advantage along with computers. We can get the information from around the world at our doorstep. These advancements are opening a wide horizon for our developments.

56. Internet

Internet is a revolutionary achievement of mankind which has changed the meaning of education. The knowledge from around the world can be gained through computers. Seeing is believing and it is also retained better. This is also the reason for the increasing popularity of computers and internet.

E-mail has made it very easy to send mails worldwide at the wink of an eye. The internet also provides a big knowledge bank in subjects like Science, Maths, Geography, Hindi, Sanskrit, German etc. You can find a live description of nature and its activities. Maps of different countries along with detailed information about their culture, people, flora and fauna is also available.

Internet has added great speed to all our activities. Internet has also benefitted people by providing access to foreign goods and an opportunity to supply their goods to foreign countries.

The internet holds the key to our bright future.

57. Disadvantages/ill effects of Science

Science has made our lives easy and comfortable. At home, office or school, science has touched every corner of our lives. It is capable of providing information about weather conditions in advance and curing the most dreaded diseases. Communication and travel have now become instant.

Along with its blessings, science has also proved to be a curse in some areas. The chemicals released as a result of industrial pollution are damaging all spheres of our environment. The chemical fertilisers and growth boosters are affecting the nutritive value of vegetables and fruits. The most dreaded discovery of science is nuclear power and the nuclear bomb. Each country is now struggling to be a bigger nuclear poser than the other.

Science has made us slaves of the various inventions. We are dependent on machines for everything. We are becoming greedy and dissatisfied. The fast developing machines are increasing unemployment. People are driving away from their traditional roots.

Though computers have eased our lives but they have also reduced our mental calibre.

It is in our hands to utilise effectively, any discovery. We should not allow advancement at the cost of degeneration of environment and brotherhood.

58. Rainbow

Nature always amazes us with its beauty and creation. On a warm sunny day, suddenly the breeze becomes cool and the bright blue sky is shadowed by grey clouds. Thundering sky brings down rain to bathe the earth.

Peacocks and birds begin to dance and children enjoy getting drenched in rain. As the rain gives way to clear weather, the seven colours of rainbow smile at us from behind the clouds. Some water droplets are left in the air after a spell of showers, when the rays of the sun fall on them, they are reflected into seven colours – violet, indigo, blue, green, yellow, orange, red.

Little children enjoy adding a rainbow to their paintings. Rainbow has also attracted many compositions and delighted all of us for generations.

59. Telephone/Mobile Phones

The telephone was invented by Alexander Graham Bell. With its invention, communication became better and news travelled faster. Today many facilities have added to this basic unit, making it fast and cheap.

Today all countries, villages and districts are connected through telephones. It is easy to communicate at far flung places. Today a village farmer is not fooled by the money lenders. He calls the market himself to know the real price for his crop.

Calling before going to meet someone has become a trend in modern era. Even if you are not available at home, people can still reach you through mobile phones. Big companies have made possible that mobile phones reach each and every corner of the country.

Generally police and intelligence departments tap phones to know anti-social activities that are being planned. Today mobile and telephone are a necessity in every house. Big and small shopkeepers also encourage free home deliveries through telephones. This invention of Graham Bell has become a lifeline of the whole world.

60. Television/DTH

Television was invented in 1926 by John L Baird of England. It is a source of recreation that satisfies the mind, eyes, ears and emotions. It shows the face of the broadcaster, the broadcasting centre etc.

From the black and white era we have travelled today to the times of DTH. Today, without the control of any cable operator, we can watch all our favourite programmes.

The dramas on the televisions are a source of recreation for women at home. Cartoons and animal related programmes satisfy the curiosity of the young minds. The television provides us live telecast of sports events from around the world. We also get to see a detailed account of national and international news.

Television has given us the remote control to the happenings around the world. It has become a big industry. The decision as to how much and what we should view still lies in our hands.

61. Newspaper

The newspapers were developed in the 16th century in Italy. Today they are a bed-tea companion in every house. Newspapers are not just a source of news from around the world, but also a big word bank to improve knowledge.

During the British rule, the revolutionaries used newspapers as a source to spread their revolutionary messages across the country. Freedom fighters like Ishwarchand Vidyasagar, Bhagat Singh, Raja Rammohan Roy brought out many newspapers in their times.

Newspapers are daily, weekly or monthly. India has regional newspapers in almost all states today. These present the social issues, business news, political and scientific developments along with advertisements.

We can also send our thoughts, poems, stories etc. in the newspapers. All papers now have a separate section for students. They also publish the events from different schools.

Newspapers are a daily dose for our minds. Even a quick reading through them enriches our mind.

Part 8 : Biographies

62. The biography of a Book

I am a Class-V Hindi Reader. Everybody respects the national language, Hindi, but Varun does not take care of me at all. Varun's parents purchased me at the beginning of the session and covered me neatly. Then I was handed over to Varun and here begins my tale of misery.

Varun keeps scribbling on my pages. He also overwrites on the beautiful pictures drawn. He enjoys adding beard and moustache to the pictures of great personalities.

Now my patience is getting exhausted. My beautiful texture has turned yellow with the oil from Varun's lunch box. At times, my pages turn and are buried under the weight of other books. Varun also enjoys running scissors across my pages.

I keep waiting to be returned to Varun's bag after the Hindi class. Children passing by hit me roughly and sometimes even drop me on the floor. If this is the punishment of being a knowledge bank, I would never want to be a book again.

Though Varun will need me in his exams. At that time I will give him my full support and prove myself to be his true companion.

63. The autobiography of a Pen

I am a long and slender blue pen. Ravi's father bought me on Basant Panchmi. It is also the day of Goddess Saraswati. He introduced me to everybody and instructed them to use me only for special tasks.

Ravi's elder sister got a project on earthquakes. She took her father's permission to use me for the same. As I wrote the stories of sufferings, I felt very sad. Then we wrote about the relief work and I felt happy to learn about noble souls who still work for the cause of humanity.

Ravi's mother composes beautiful poems. I proudly shoulder the responsibility of putting into words the music of rivers, the hustle of the trees and the chirping of birds. I feel great about my contribution to literature.

Ravi also takes me along for his examination. Then I dutifully write without stopping.

Ravi's father uses me in his account books. I feel scared at that time and work with maximum concentration.

The experience of writing so many subjects is making me very knowledgeable.

64. The autobiography of a Flower

I am a part of the vast nature, I am a rose flower. I am a red and fragrant flower, a part of many poetic compositions. Pt. Nehru always adorned me on his coat.

I live on the branches amidst many thorns. In an attempt to pluck me, your fingers might get pricked. It gives you an important lesson in life that to achieve attractive goals, you will have to pass through many obstacles.

I am also used as a beauty product. 'Gulab Jal' is a beauty source in itself. Many queens have bathed in it for youthful skin.

Events like marriage, prayers or condolence never accomplish without me. I watch political rallies sitting around the necks of political leaders. I have become very knowledgeable about our country politics.

After all this respect endowed upon me, when I begin to wither, I am thrown in a dustbin. If you rather throw me in a lawn or garden, I would happily serve as manure to my friends.

65. The autobiography of a Bag

I am a green coloured bag with two zips. I am proud of my shiny surface. Though I am old, my surface is clean and fresh. Rahul takes very good care of me. He cleans the pictures of spiderman on my front pocket everyday.

My front pocket provides space to carry lunch. Rahul always carries his tiffin box in a brown bag to avoid spilling. Every morning he dusts me before setting the books.

I sit along with Sahil's bag. His bag narrates a different story. It smells of oil. Sahil clumsily drops it on the floor all the time and I helplessly watch it.

On the shoulders of an intelligent child, holding knowledgeable books, I look at the world with pride. I take a bath every Saturday evening. Soon, it will be time for Rahul to move to the next class. Then, he will buy a new bag. I wonder where I would go then!

66. The autobiography of a Library

I am the house of books, a library. I have a huge collection of books on Science, Geography, Hindi, English, Maths, stories and pictures. I belong to the primary wing of a famous school. I am located at the first floor. I welcome the students with open arms into my world of books.

The students understand that I like discipline and silence. Therefore, they follow the rules carefully. They place the books at the right place after using them. They make me very happy when they pull the chairs very slowly.

All the students have been given two cards – one is red and the other green. The red card allows books to be issued for only one day. The green card allows the books to be issued for a week.

I get worried when students of class V-D come for their library period. This class is notorious for misplacing and manhandling books. Constant whispering and noise of chairs marks their presence. The librarian himself inspects their class.

Disciplined and organised children always keep the books properly and return them on time. I also like such students.

67. The autobiography of a Garden

I am a garden. I am the playground for fresh air, flowers, bees and butterflies. I am located in Mohan Nagar. A soft carpet of green grass and a magnificent rock garden mark my entry with a big board of 'Mohan Nagar Welfare Committee' that welcomes you.

Though I am very old, my reconstruction and maintenance has been taken up by this committee just two years ago. They have beautifully landscaped my area. New grass and rows of beautiful flowers, fountains and lighting have given me a new look. Now, I feel very proud in welcoming everyone. There is a three meter broad track for walkers and joggers. One round equals one kilometer. The sprawling lawns around the track are ideal for exercise. Two of these lawns have swings for children. I enjoy it when the children jump around these swings. An army of four gardeners and four helpers constantly work to remove dried leaves, plants and insects. The members of the committee come for regular inspection.

I am being taken care like a little baby and I am also enjoying the many colours of nature.

Part 9 : Our Environment

68. Pollution

Where on one hand the development programmes today are breaking all boundaries, on the other hand it is leaving behind a dirty trail of pollution.

Nature gifted us with a balanced environment. The cycle of seasons followed its time and there was a fixed amount of all components in nature. The human activities have severely upset the balance of nature through constant scientific experiments.

The water bodies have now become a source of chemicals, oil spillage and sewage from cities and industries. Lately we have witnessed large numbers of dead sea animals washed away at the shores.

The smoke left by vehicles, industries and nuclear experiments is constantly degrading the environment. The unlimited deforestation has upset the oxygen balance of nature. It has also caused a decrease in the amount of rainfall received per annum.

Human beings are falling prey to many cancerous diseases including respiratory, skin and digestive disorders.

Though the government is constantly working towards control of pollution but it is not possible without our cooperation. We can help by afforestation, banning the use of polythene and the right disposal of waste.

69. Our Forests

The dense, green forests are a rich source of fuel, food, wood, medicine and clean environment. They play a very important role in maintaining balance in nature.

The roots of the trees bind within them many important nutrients of the soil. They also act as a hurdle for floods. The trees house many rare and beautiful species of birds and animals. These also serve as tourist spots when declared as sanctuaries and National parks.

The forests regulate rainfall, making the land more fertile. The products like wood, gum, resins, honey, herbs etc. are the raw material for many industries. A wide variety of wood like sal, sheesham, teak can be obtained from the woods, used for building and construction.

To avoid indiscriminate deforestation for human use, the government is now taking stern measures. There are strict rules against cutting trees and hunting as well. Chipko Movement was an exceptional movement to save forests.

70. Floods

The increasing thirst for development is leading to permanent damages in nature.

The indiscriminate cutting of trees is causing a change in the passage of rivers, their flow is also becoming uncontrolled. The result is floods.

Floods are generally caused by excessive rains though at times less rain added to the above reasons can also be a cause. The water flows without control breaking through the banks of river during floods. It takes along the plantation, crops, and livestock.

A big metropolitan like Mumbai is also coming under floods every year now. Floods has been causing a great loss of life and property there. The amount of water rose to two storeys at many places. Transportation, telephone, electricity, everything came to a stand still.

People get stuck due to water logging. The sewage water mixes with drinking water, polluting it and spreading diseases.

To avoid instances like this it is important to plant trees along the river banks and build dams. We should help government and non-government agencies to work towards forest conservation.

71. Earthquake

Many activities constantly take place inside the core of the earth. We never come to know of these movements on the surface. The centre of the earth is made up of molten lava. The layers above it are also disturbed by the heat of this lava. When this disturbance is felt on the topmost layers, it is called an earthquake.

The tremors due to the earthquake are generally felt for three to five seconds and are measured on an instrument called Richter Scale. An earthquake measuring above 5 is supposed to be destructive.

Earthquakes cause big building to fall into pieces, at places cracks appear in the ground. Many people collapse under the weight of the rubble.

The most difficult job after an earthquake is to dig out people safely from the rubble. Earthquakes render many homeless. We should donate liberally for their food, clothing, medicines etc.

72. The Sunrise

The sun energises the earth with its heat and light. Its rays are a source of life on earth. The seasons also change according to the distance of the earth from the sun.

The sun always rises from the east. The night shadows are quietly washed away by the bright morning sun. The warm orange rays spread across the sky until the stars disappear behind the clear blue sky.

As the sun slowly appears from the horizon, its immense energy vitalises the mind and body. Indian saints and sages have attached great value to offering prayers to the rising sun. It helps us imbibe the sun's energy within us.

Not just humans but even birds enjoy the vast expanse of the sky with the rising sun. The sunflower cheers up and smiles at the east.

Sunrise inspires us for a new beginning every morning.

Part 10 : Thought Related

73. Students and Discipline

Discipline connects humans with social norms. Human beings are governed by rules in all spheres of their lives. These rules apply in studies, sports, socialising, clubs etc. Working within these rules is discipline.

The students are the next generation of the society. They will take their country to new horizons. An undisciplined child is an easy target for social evils. Disrespecting elders, dishonouring teachers, not following a routine, not cooperating with friends while playing and studying, these are all characteristics of an undisciplined child.

The family is the first school to learn discipline norms. The children naturally pick up good habits from their families. The schools discipline children by providing opportunities for mental and physical development.

Disciplined students are an asset to the nation and they help in the progress of a country. Discipline develops more with self control than external control.

Discipline implies giving up your bad habits and accepting good habits to make your life better and meaningful.

74. Hardwork

Lethargy is the biggest human enemy. It is an obstacle to any activity in our life. Lethargy makes a man inactive and dulls his mind as well. One does not get everything on a platter. We have to work for it. Even the tiger has to hunt for its food. Nature does not offer it food easily. Thus, hard work is the only key to success.

We depend on hard work to fulfill our desires in life. India gained freedom from the British rule only because of the hardwork of her freedom fighters. Our literature has also been enriched by the continuous efforts of great composers like Sarojini Naidu, Mahadevi Verma, Rabindranath Tagore and the others. The great warriors like Maharaja Ranjeet Singh, Shivaji, Rana Pratap have earned their fame with extreme hardwork.

People do not admit their laziness and often blame destiny for their failure. In schools, we are taught the importance of hardwork in all spheres. Thus, we should make hardwork a way of life.

75. Good Behaviour

Good behaviour is the biggest wealth of a person. Good behaviour earns a person high status in society as well as well as success in all spheres. A person with good conduct has a calm mind and he is also able to accomplish all his tasks well.

The primary characteristics of an honest person are honesty, non-violence, faith in God, love and respect for fellow beings. Lord Rama was a virtuous person. He greeted everyone with love and respect. But Ravana earned a bad name when he kidnapped Sita.

Virtuous people never do anything wrong and thus, they are not afraid of anything. They keep themselves in good company and good atmosphere. They prove their words through their deeds.

A virtuous student is one who has the qualities of hardwork, soft speech, love, respect for elders and friendly behaviour. By inculcating these values we make place for ourselves amongst our friends and elders. We stay happy and it also improves our work quality.

76. Good Company

A man is known by the company he keeps. Our friends and company guide our life to a great extent. Good company means the company of virtuous people. Their good thoughts influence our own thoughts as well.

Good company is like the golden touch of midas. It makes our lives bright and invaluable like gold. On the other hand, the bad thoughts of our friends makes us to think and behave in wrong way.

We can learn a lot from good company. Their routine, their interest in books and sports and their performance in studies also inspires us to work hard. Good company illuminates our lives like the torch.

We carry our childhood habits throughout our lives, hence we should be very careful about the friends we choose and the habits we pick up from them.

77. Best use of Time

Time is a valuable possession. It never comes back. We may lose and find many things again but such is not the case with time.

We have to make the best use of time available to us to finish our work according to a routine. Using our spare time to learn something new is an effective use of time. By understanding how to manage our time wisely, we can climb high on the ladder of success.

People who waste time and not manage it wisely are generally left out of the race. They keep repenting and blaming destiny. Great inventors like James Watt, Madam Curie, Addison, all worked hard, round the clock, to become great achievers.

The sun, the earth, the moon and the seasons, all follow time. The seasons are enjoyed best when they come at the right time.

Student life is a phase when one learns the most. We learn amazing, new things about the world, sports, Science, etc. Thus, whatever time we have, we should use it effectively to achieve success in studies and co-curricular activities.

78. Our National Language – Hindi

Language is the foremost means to exchange ideas. All countries have their own special traditions, literature, knowledge pool and language. Hindi is the national language of India. It is written in Devanagri script.

The national language is the one which is spoken and understood in most parts of the country. A few regional changes cause the language to branch out into forms. All the official and government communication is taken up in the national language.

On 14 September 1949, Hindi was declared the national language of our country. A few other languages like Sanskrit, Tamil, Telugu, Punjabi etc. also got recognition. Hindi has a rich literary heritage. For ages, ancient scholars have used Hindi as a means to express stories, poetry, and ancient wisdom. Great achievers like Aryabhatt also used Hindi as a medium to express their discoveries.

Some people consider Hindi to be a very simple language. They believe it to be incompetent in the modern world. They vote for English instead. But the national language represents the culture and tradition of every country. We should also feel proud conversing in Hindi as we would feel for any other foreign language.

79. Increasing Population

Today the biggest problem facing the independent, developing India is its increasing population. The other related problems are poverty and unemployment. Every single minute, about 47 babies are born.

The resources remain the same and the load of population on these resources is increasing. This is reducing the pace of development.

The problem is more in the illiterate section because they believe in 'more children, more hands to work'. The literate section, unfortunately, wants a male child and hence keeps adding numbers to their family till a male child is born.

The evils of increasing population are increasing diseases, corruption, inflation, crime etc.

We can save ourselves from these problems by considering girl and boy to be equal and restricting to a small family. A small population can gain the maximum from the country's resources.

80. Corruption

Corruption is a termite which eats away the very foundation of a nation. It includes bribery, treachery and dishonesty.

Corruption is a tool for the immoral people. Such people care only for their selfish interest.

Many of our democratic leaders have a long crime record including violence, kidnapping etc. The shopkeepers do not weigh correctly or bill properly. They also add adulterated toxins to dried cereals and grains to increase the weight. These can be very harmful for our health.

The police personnel or government officials have often been caught taking bribes. Unfortunately, corrupt people can also be seen within the hospitals. Such immoral people create big problems for the nation.

Corrupt people are not concerned about feelings of nationhood or social cause. The progress of a country slows down because of immoral and corrupt people.

The students have a huge responsibility to shoulder to stop such people and give our society a new and better foundation.

81. Nationhood

Our nation, our motherland, nourishes us like a mother. Our country provides us the food and resources for our all round development, making our lives prosperous.

It is our duty to nurture feelings of love and respect for our country. This develops a feeling of belongingness to the nation, the feeling of nationhood. These emotions are beyond self and inspire us to accept the good and bad aspects of our country.

We can repay our motherland with a few simple gestures. Saving resources, like electricity and water, keeping our environment neat and clean, not felling trees but planting more trees, not littering on the roads, following rules etc.

If we are blessed with wealth, then we must always use it for the welfare of the needy. We should aid in the National Literacy Mission.

We should understand the reasons for backwardness of our country. We should make people aware of the futility of superstitions and help our society progress. Only a literate and scientifically aware citizen can understand the true meaning of nationhood.

82. Stories/Story Reading

Our mind has an amazing capacity to learn. It is the playground for imagination. Though, we should not live in a dream world, but imagination gives birth to creativity. Art forms like painting, dance, music, sculptures, story writing, etc. are possible only with creative imagination.

We all read stories in our childhood. Stories have two advantages – first, they enrich our language and second, we learn many new things and become one with the writer's thinking.

The characters of the story take us on an adventure trip along with them and also inspire us to think positive. Like all the stories from Panchatantra end in a moral for us to learn. The collection of short stories 'Malgudi Days' by R.K. Narayan describe childhood adventures of a village boy.

Many great story writers have enriched our literature with great works. Premchand presents the hardships of life using the writing form called a 'satire'. Tagore has written many stories which are an inspiration to the students. Stories are a source of recreation for us children. They keep us stress free and enthused.

83. Our National Symbols

All countries have certain symbols which are unique to them, and which form their individuality like its flag, flowers, birds etc. There is a uniqueness in declaring these symbols as national symbols.

Our national flag is called the Tricolour. The first colour of our flag is saffron. It signifies sacrifice, bravery and nationalism. The white colour in the centre stands for peace and the third colour, green signifies our agriculture and prosperity. The white colour also bears a deep blue 'chakra' with 24 spokes. It signifies the 24 hours in a day.

Our National Anthem, 'Jana Gana Mana', was composd by Shri Rabindranath Tagore. It was declared our National Anthem on 24 January, 1950.

Tiger is our National Animal and peacock is our National Bird. The lotus has been declared our National Flower and mango is our National Fruit. Mango is also called the 'King of Fruits' and is rich in vitamin A, C and D.

The Banyan tree is our National Tree. We should respect our national symbols. We should always stand up to honour our national flag whenever it is hoisted and whenever our national anthem is sung. It speaks a great deal about the strength of our character and love for our country.

Part 11 : Great Personalities

84. Gautam Buddha

'Buddha' means the one with an enlightened mind. Gautam Buddha is one of the great inspirations and teachers of the world.

Buddha was born in Nepal and was named 'Siddhartha' by his parents. At his birth, astrologers predicted that he will renounce the world. Since then his father kept him amidst great luxuries.

When he grew up, he had a deep desire to see the outside world. On his way he saw a dead body, an old man and an ill person. Not having known pain, Siddhartha was depressed to see the three facts of life. His father married him off to Yashodhara and they had a son Rahul.

Siddharth gave up all luxuries to live as an ascetic at the age of 29. For the next 45 years he wandered from one place to another preaching love, brotherhood and sacrifice. His followers increased in numbers and 'Buddhism' was established as a new way of life.

He left for heavenly abode at the age of 80 years.

85. Guru Nanak Devji

Guru Nanak Devji was the founder of Sikh religion. He was born on the 15th April 1469. The astrologers predicted his interests in religion. They also said that he would be regarded by Hindus and Muslims alike.

Guru Nanak Devji was never interested in money matters. Once his father sent him out with twenty rupees for business. On his way, he fed a few saints and returned home. Similarly, whenever he was put in business ventures, he ended up spending money on the needy.

He was married at the age of eighteen and had two sons. But he was not a worldly man. He went out in search of truth and to help the distressed. He propagated his principles all around the country. His disciples organised 'langars' which spread the concept of one kitchen for all.

Guru Nanak Devji combined the best ideologies of the Hindu and Muslim religion and gave them the form of Sikhism. He composed the 'Japuji Saheb' for morning prayers and 'Rehraas Saheb' for evening prayers.

At the age of 70 years, in the year 1538, he left for heavenly abode. His philosophies and teachings were taken forth and spread everywhere by his disciple Angad, who also came to be known as Guru Angad Devji.

86. Swami Vivekanand

India is a country of Saints. Our culture has been blessed by the verses of many divine souls. They have guided us on the path to devotion and selflessness.

Swami Vivekanand, a great saint was born on 12 January 1863 in Kolkata. He was named Narendranath at birth. He was a sharp and obedient student with deep interest in studies.

Swamiji was a student of Shri Ramakrishna Paramhansa. He spread Ramakrishna's message across the whole country. His principles promoted progress of man and not superstitions.

He gave many lectures on religion which influenced people all over the world. His famous book 'Rajyog' is popular among people even today. He established 'Ramakrishna Mission' at two different places in Kolkata.

He was a strong critic of social evils. Due to long working hours and diabetes, he died on 4th July 1902. His teachings are still a guiding lamp for us.

87. Bankim Chandra Chattopadhyay

Bankim Chandra Chattopadhyay is a great name in Indian History who gave us the slogan of 'Vande Mataram'. He was a great writer of the 19th century India. He had immense leadership qualities.

He was born on 26th June, 1838 in Bengal. He was an intelligent and courageous boy. He joined a British Office soon after graduation. But his anger against them began to get reflected in his writings. He wrote many novels and stories in Bangla. He also started a monthly magazine in Bangla by the name 'Bangadarshan'.

His rebellious novel 'Anandmath' reflected great anger against the British rule. This novel added fuel to the already fuming war of independence. The slogan 'Vande Mataram' was first used in this novel and it later began to be heard from every corner of the country.

Bankim spent his whole life writing on social and political issues. He also attacked the social evils like child marriage, sati etc. with his pen.

He was given the title of 'Rai Bahadur'. Bankim breathed his last on 8th April 1894.

88. Rabindranath Tagore

Born on 8th May 1861 in Kolkata, Tagore was a great poet, painter, dramatist and composer. He is better known for his contribution as a freedom fighter in the war of independence.

He was born as the fourteenth child of Maharishi Devendranath. His family was honoured with the title of 'Thakurs' by the British Government. He lost his mother, Sharda Devi, in childhood. With a busy father, he learnt to grow up independently. This phase of his life can be seen in his sensitive and touching poems.

Tagore wrote extensively on religion, science, music, social reforms and many other subjects.

He was awarded the Nobel Prize for his literary contribution 'Geetanjali' on 13 November, 1913. With the money from the Nobel Prize, he established the 'Vishwabharti' University popularly called 'Shantiniketan'. He also composed our National Anthem 'Jana Gana Mana'.

89. Chandrashekhar Azad

Chandrashekhar Azad is a name in the independence struggle that stands as a similie for courage, bravery and discipline. He was born in an ordinary family in the Jhabua district of Madhya Pradesh. He was never interested in studies.

At the time of the Jallianwala Bagh incident, he was about eleven years old. The Britishers fired indiscriminately at the helpless children, women and old people, who had gathered for a silent protest at the Jallianwala Bagh. Chandrashekhar Azad was deeply shocked by this incident and he plunged into the freedom struggle at a very tender age.

As he grew up, so did his anger against the British. He was a master in disguising and tricked the British many times. They were unable to catch him.

He joined and led many revolutionary parties. He gave a new definition to the war of independence. Once caught amidst British soldiers, he shot himself, not letting the enemy touch his body.

90. Rani Laxmibai

Rani Laxmibai was born in 1830 in Banaras in a well off family. She was called 'Manu' and she trained herself in riding, weapons etc. at a young age.

She was married to King Gangadhar at a tender age of fourteen. Then on she came to be known as Rani Laxmibai.

At that time the British was forcing the rulers to sign a treaty. According to it, if a king died without a natural heir, his throne would be taken over by the British. Gangadhar Rao's state was also bound by a similar treaty. He died without an heir. Rani Laxmibai adopted Damodar Rai but British government refused to accept him as the heir.

Rani Laxmibai sought help from many neighbouring states, fighting numerous battles against British. She died fighting the British in one of the battles, but is praised even today for her bravery.

91. Ishwarchandra Vidyasagar

Ishwarchandra Vidyasagar was born in a poor Bengali family on 28 September, 1820. His mother was Bhagwati Devi and father was Thakurdas Bandhopadhya. They were simple and kind hearted people.

Ishwarchandra was sent to school at the age of 5. He was a brilliant student, praised by all. He had an amazing memory.

After graduation he was appointed as a lecturer in Fort William College at Kolkata. Ishwarchandra always detested British rule. He was a benevolent and self-reliant person. Once on his visit to a British officer, he was not offered a seat. He left quietly and repeated the same with the officer on his visit. The angry Britisher summoned him. He politely replied that he was merely imitating civilsed people. This incident became an example of his self-respect.

He worked for the education of the backward classes and protested against evils like child marriage, caste system, atrocities on women and the poor, and many others. Ishwarchandra Vidyasagar is known as a great social reformer of his time.

92. Kalpana Chawla

Kalpana Chawla was born in the year 1961 in Karnal district of Haryana. Since childhood she idolised Shri J.R.D. Tata. She completed her schooling from Tagore Public School and finished her degree in Aeronautics from Punjab University.

In 1982, she went to America for higher education. There she began to work with NASA. In 1997, she was selected for the first time for a space mission. She took her first space flight in a spaceship called Columbia. She made a record of being 360 hours in space.

In July 2002, she went for her second space mission. This time she carried along a white satin flag, as a mark of respect for her teachers.

On February 1, 2003, her spaceship blew up and was destroyed while entering the earth's atmosphere. None of the seven astronauts survived.

She was awarded many honours posthumously. She enjoyed watching birds, reading and flying. She used to call the whole world her nation and she proved it.

93. Pratibha Patil

Pratibha Patil is the first woman President of India. She was born on 19 December, 1934 in Nandgaon, Maharashtra. After completing her schooling, she graduated in law from Government Law College, Mumbai.

She was a good table tennis player. She was also awarded the title of 'College Queen' in 1962 by M.J. College.

Smt Patil started her political career in 1962 as a Congress M.P. She was greatly influenced by Indira Gandhi. She held many important posts. She was also the Governor of Rajasthan from November 2004 till June 2007.

Pratibha Patil is the twelfth President of India. Her husband Devi Singh Shekhawat is a teacher. Together they established many schools and universities in Jalgaon. They also started a 'Shram Sadhna' Trust for working women.

On 25 July, 2007, she took over as the President of India. She is an example for the women of our country.

94. Subhash Chandra Bose

A revolutionary was born on 23 January, 1897 in Cuttack, Orissa. His father Janakidas Bose and mother Prabhavati instilled spiritual and moral qualities in him since childhood. Netaji Subhash Chandra Bose was highly influenced by Swami Vivekanand. He was more influenced by the ideas of Shri Lokmanya Tilak and Shri Aurobindo though a little less by Mahatma Gandhi.

He got into the freedom struggle and his slogan "Give me blood and I will give you freedom" became the motivation for all youth. He worked for India's freedom and joined Congress to support his struggle. He was even nominated the President of Congress. But he soon found his way of working was different from their ideology, so he left Congress.

He formed the Indian National Army (INA) in 1941 which continued its struggle against the British in the North-Eastern region of India. The chief aim of INA was to push out British Army from North-East states and take them to Delhi, and fight them there. Thus, their slogan was 'Dilli Chalo'.

On 17th August 1945, Netaji was killed in an aircraft accident. His slogan 'Jai Hind' still inspires the Indians.

Part 12 : Sight Seeing

95. Taj Mahal

Taj Mahal is located on the banks of river Yamuna in Agra. It is one of the seven wonders of the world. It is made of white marble and stands as a symbol of love of King Shahjahan for his wife Mumtaz.

Taj Mahal was a result of the hard labour of twenty thousand labourers. It is also famous for its unique carving. A big gate made of red stone welcomes us to this beautiful monument. A stream of clear water guides the straight path from the gate to the monument. Many fountains decorate this stream with carpets of green grass on either side.

There are four towers at the four corners of the Taj. As you reach the terrace, the view is more amazing. On one side you can see the Yamuna river and on the other is the Agra city. In the centre is a big tomb.

There are two graves inside Taj Mahal. These graves bear beautiful carvings with gems and precious stones, displaying floral motifs, which can be also seen on all the walls and entrances. Below the two graves, in the basement of Taj Mahal, are the actual graves of Shahjahan and Mumtaz.

Taj Mahal is a famous tourist spot and its re-entry into the seven wonders expresses our love towards it.

96. Rashtrapati Bhawan

Rashtrapati Bhawan is the official accomodation of the President of India. Beautifully trimmed trees and rows of colourful flowers outline this huge structure.

It used to be the house of the Viceroy before independence. In 1952 after the Republic Day, it was declared as the President's House.

The Rashtrapati Bhawan is spread out in an area of one kilometre and was built over a period of 17 years by the hardwork of 3500 masons.

The entry of the Rashtrapati Bhawan leads to a big hall which is made of coloured marble. It has golden-coloured pillars.

The famous Mughal Gardens is the President's personal lawn which is open to the public during the spring season in February-March. The rare species of flowers are aesthetically arranged. The spring seems to be dressed in its best here.

Right across the Rashtrapati Bhawan stands India Gate. It is a memorial built to honour the freedom fighters.

The Republic Day parade on 26th January begins from the Rashtrapati Bhawan and walking down the Rajpath, it ends at India Gate. The Rashtrapati Bhawan is also decorated with lights on this day.

97. Qutub Minar

Qutub Minar is a 239 feet tall monument, situated in New Delhi. It is the tallest building of India.

Qutub Minar has five storeys. The first three storeys are constructed in red stone and the other two are made of marble. The history of the structure is also carved here.

An entrance to the north leads to the stairs. A flight of 379 steps separates each floor.

Erected in 1199 by Emperor Qutubuddin Aibak, this structure has withstood many tremors and shocks from earthquakes and lightning. In 1368, the two storeys on the top were reduced to shambles by lightning. They were reconstructed by Sultan Sikander Lodhi. In 1803, the whole monument was shaken by a major earthquake. It was repaired by Major R. Smith of the ruling British Government.

The area around the monument has sprawling lawns which are a favourite picnic spot. The Ashoka Pillar adjacent to it is also a major tourist attraction.

This beautiful monument with its unique structure and beautiful architecture, is my favourite tourist spot.

98. Red Fort

Red Fort is a beautiful piece of architecture constructed by the great emperor Shahjahan. It is located on the Western banks of river Yamuna in Old Delhi.

Constructed in red stone, it stands tall in praise of the Mughal architecture.

The construction of this grand fort began in the year 1638 and took 9 years to complete. It was the palace of Emperor Shahjahan. At that time Delhi was his capital and it was known as Shahjahanabad. The market around the fort was built for the purpose of trade and was called Chandni Chowk. The country men lived in this market.

The Red Fort had big rooms, with marble flooring and the market for the royals. Inside the fort is a mosque and the beauty of lawns and fountains still attract many visitors. To make the fort secure, it was given a 60 foot high boundary wall.

Our first Prime Minister Pandit Jawaharlal Nehru hoisted our National Flag at the Red Fort soon after independence. Since then on every 15th August, the Prime Minister addresses the whole nation from the Red Fort.

The Red Fort houses a war museum and a museum displaying events of our independence movement. The paintings from Mughal period, their clothing and utility items, displayed in the museum still look lively and new.

LETTER WRITING

We express our feelings, thoughts and invitations to our friends and relatives through letters. We use letters for official work too.

While writing letters, one should concentrate on the following points:

1. The language of the letter should be clear and easy.
2. The correct words for greeting and ending should be used.
3. The address and date should be at the right place. It is most important for official letters.
4. The name of the person and address should be legibly written on the envelope.

Salutation and Subscription

Salutation – Respected (for elders), My Dear, Dear (for friends)

Subscription – Yours affectionately/lovingly/obediently, Yours loving

Official Letters

Salutation – Sir, Madam

Subscription – Yours faithfully, Yours Sincerely

Part 1 : Official Letters/Business Letters

1. Leave Application

The Principal
D.A.V. School,
Sector 22, Dwarka,
New Delhi

Subject : Application for five days leave

Respected Sir,

With due respect I wish to inform that my brother's marriage has been fixed for 30th April, 2009. Kindly grant me leave from 29th April to 3rd May for five days and oblige.

Thanking you,

Yours faithfully

Sunil Kumar
Class V A

5 February, 2009

2. Application for Fee Concession

The Principal
Gyan Devi School
Patel Chowk,
New Delhi

Subject : Application for Fee Concession

Respected Sir,

With due respect I wish to explain the adverse circumstances at home. My father is a small government official. My mother is suffering from serious illness and needs expensive treatment. My younger sister is also a student at a government school. In such a condition I am unable to pay my school fee.

I have excelled in my studies every year. I would request you to grant me fee concession and oblige.

Thanking you,

Yours faithfully

Aashish Sharma
Class V C

3 February, 2009

3. Letter to order books from a book store

The Manager
Scholars Hub
B-11, Lajpat Nagar,
New Delhi

Respected Sir,

Kindly send the following books through VPP at the address given below.

Name of the book	**Copies**
1. My First Dictionary	4 copies
2. Mental Maths Part II	3 copies
3. World Maps	6 copies

I hope the books will be sent in good condition and at a concessional rate.

Thanking you,

Yours faithfully

Meenakshi Dhar
5, Kirti Nagar
New Delhi

17 February, 2009

4. Application for opening a Bank Account

The Manager
Punjab National Bank
Naya Bazar, Surat
Gujarat

Subject: Opening a new Bank Account

Respected Sir,

With due respect I wish to open a joint saving account with my mother Mrs. Rama Sharma in your branch. The copy of our ration card along with two passport size photographs each are attached alongwith. Kindly open the account at the earliest and help us avail the facilities provided by your bank.

Thanking you,

Yours faithfully

Ranjana Sharma
2/7, Naya Bazar, Surat
Gujarat

23 January, 2009

5. Application to the Traffic Police Department for installation of Traffic Signal at the crossing

Assistant Traffic Commissioner
Central Area
New Delhi

Subject: Installation of traffic signal

Respected Sir,

With due respect I wish to draw your attention to the main crossing in Chandni Chowk. The traffic has increased in the past three years leading to confusion and accidents. I request you to install a traffic signal and ease the movement of the traffic.

Awaiting an early reaction.

Thanking you,

Yours faithfully

Shishu Kumar
President,
RWA,
Chandni Chowk,
Delhi-110006

25 January, 2009

Part 2 : Unofficial/Personal Letters

1. Letter to your father listing your achievements in sports

J-138,
Rajouri Garden,
New Delhi

8 February, 2009

Respected father,

I was glad to receive your letter. It was nice to hear that you all are keeping well.

I am coping well with my studies and sports. I am strictly following your advice on regular exercise. I have established myself well in the cricket team here. I am regular with my practice sessions. My coach has signalled me to be the next captain.

Rest is all well. Give my regards to mother and love to Ritu.

Yours obediently

Subhash

2. Invitation to a friend for sister's marriage

5/17, Panchsheel Bhawan,
Chanakyapuri,
New Delhi

9 January, 2009

Dear Rajni,

I am glad to inform you that my sister's marriage has been fixed for 15th January. The ceremony will be organised in a community hall near our house. You must come two days in advance for Sangeet and Mehandi. We will have fun together.

The details of the programme are given in the card enclosed.

Waiting for your reply.

Your dear friend

Neera

3. Letter to congratulate your friend on scoring well in exams

C-161,
Mathura Road,
New Delhi

28 November, 2008

Dear Amit,

I received your letter. I was very happy to know you scored well in the half-yearly exams. The credit for your success goes to your hard work and determination. I wish you success at every step in your life.

With best wishes

Your dear friend

Pranav

4. Letter of condolence to your friend

House No. 4,
Shipra Apartments
Ghaziabad

11 January, 2009

Dear Gauri,

I received your letter. Though I knew about your grandmother's illness but the news of the sudden demise was very shocking. We all had been blessed by her love and affection. I sincerely pray for her soul to rest in peace. My heartfelt sympathy will always be with you and your family.

Your friend

Riya

5. Letter to your younger brother explaining advantages of keeping good company

4/53,
Gurukripa Apartments
New Delhi-110024

Dear brother Indra,

I received father's letter. It was a shock to hear about your suspension from school. Brother, this is the age where you will make many friends. You will have to yourself select what kind of friends you should have. We all are affected by the good and bad qualities of our friends. Bad company eclipses our lives and good company enlightens it. Thus, you must be very careful in selecting friends.

Give my regards to mother and father and take care of yourself.

Your brother

Shrey

STORY WRITING

We all enjoy reading and telling stories. Stories teach us new things. They are inspiring and encouraging. They also strengthen our vocabulary and enhance our creativity.

While writing stories, the language should be clear and easy. The reader should feel himself/herself to be a part of the story while reading it.

Given below are a few stories with their outline. Pictures have been added to make them more attractive.

Pigeons and the Net

A group of pigeons was flying in search of food. Few grains of rice spread out on the ground attracted their attention. The pigeons flew down and started pecking on the grains. A wise old pigeon among them suspected foul play and warned the others that the grains could not have been there without reason. But others completely ignored his advice.

Soon, when they had their fill, the pigeons started flying again. But alas! They found themselves caught in the hunter's net. The pigeons got scared. The hunter would kill them. They tried flapping their wings in despair but with no result. The wise old pigeon spoke again. He told everyone to be calm, and then fly up – together. The pigeons took his advice seriously. They all made an effort and together flapped their wings and flew up. As they did so, the net also flew up with them. The hunter tried to catch them, but in vain. The old pigeon took his group to the little mouse, his friend. The mouse quickly cut the net with his sharp teeth and freed his friends.

Moral: Unity is strength.

Outline of stories for practice

1. The Blue Jackal

A jackal — searching for food — falls in the dyer's drum — comes out blue — reflection water — idea — calls himself the king — animals scared — follow his orders — bring him gifts — one night jackal forgets — begins to howl — his game is over.

Moral: Fraud people always end up trapped.

2. The Imitating Monkey

Carpenter in the village — working under a tree — a monkey watching carefully — lunch time — carpenter leave — monkey quickly comes down — tries to imitate — tail gets stuck between logs of wood — cries for help — carpenter rushes to his rescue.

Moral: Never imitate others.

3. Unity is Strength

A farmer — four sons — kept quarreling — once farmer — very ill — called his sons — gave them one stick each — asked them to break — then gave them a bunch of sticks — none could break — gave them a lesson — united — face any enemy — sons began to live together.

Moral: Unity is Strength.

4. Two Foolish Cats

Two cats — found one chapati — fighting — monkey watching — came down for help — divided it into two — one part was bigger — took a bite — now the second part was bigger — took another bite — soon ate the whole chapati — thanked the cats.

Moral: Third person always benefits from a fight between two people.